Dancing Over the Void

Richard MacNeill

When the summer starts
I will be a sun

Don't fall prey to the new

       seek what stays

Poets feel they are at
  the end of something
  and the beginning of something

The current renaissance, antiquity, divination

※

The daylight is all the news he needs
the writing comfort
the adventurous pondering
Stars tell us that we have been freed
no longer entrenched in arguing with walls
the elf's anger dissipates
The silence in escaping
home to remembering
the reason why is shown
No more to wit's embracing end
but the river imagined in invisible bends
The bard's hello silently singing
in the forest on a hill
in solitude's meaning
When they ask where you go
and why alone
why not join the fray of majestic bones
he may tell them when he cares to answer
though he knows they will not see
what he says
He doesn't want to live that way
and when conversations without him
rage into a stupor of careless need
he'll step back and turn to see
in the place where trees breathe
away from the bells of voices throwing
the boredom of the bourgeoisie
Slipping away, walking out
of society's fortress
to where he's been found
moving unbound, exploring the open
returned to the realm of the free

You brought the fire back to the hearth

You brought the fire back from its end
You renewed the soil and revived my hands
You called our friends back from the night
Children laughing, playing with old toys
I return to have fun and recall
what we have, paradise
what isn't missing, happiness
You reminded me to sow the purpose
You killed loneliness
The work of our dreams is our dream

※

The ancient poetry is why we live
The closely carved oxbone comb
is beautiful because it is so old
is beautiful because it is useful
is beautiful because it is cared for
The ancient red stones with hands sprayed forever
call to us because they live
We will always understand them
and language is not necessary here
It is the Sound of living

※

The mountain spoke,
Keep going. Don't give up.

Let the mountain help you
Let the mountain humble you
Remember how to breathe
pacing yourself through pain
which goes beyond pain

Silence
above the noise
where gods meditate
their pipe smoke drifting into clouds

For a moment
what was closest to the sun
were raised glasses of whisky
and the closest to the moon
were our eyes
and the pain is gone

A big wild something
tracks us on the way down
and we listen, ready
Something big passed through
behind us
we see the ripped tree
which on the way up was whole
could be a lion, a bear, or a man

Home, happy to hear the voices of love
All is well
Let me do what can only be good
let me live each day
fully understanding what is true

Abandoned

It is apparent
expectation is a norm of turmoil.
You tried to hold together
what mocks your attempted gathering
and gives no effort to love beyond ease.
Ingénues asking for flowers
to validate their egos' diluted attention
confusing the world as a servant
to their desires while shoving away
as enemies any who disagree
or confront the causes of pain.
There is lack of conversation
on both sides
making war of opinions, all of you
unaware an opinion based on lies
is not an opinion, it is misunderstanding
subjective rulership of disappearing vapor.
Go ahead and abandon those who love you
when they don't say what you want to hear
become a sad drip of a person
raised by strangers in screens
giving sympathy to your self-serving cause
abandoned by parents
in the other room
who are also attached to screens
yet nothing excuses absence of empathy.
Earthquakes disrupt your vacation
and the family who treats with royal care
and keeps the tongue bitten at your arrogance
is shunned.

※

Riding a bike through different realms
different times and paths
strange and familiar
on the highway crushing you
with time
running and preparing
until the battle
when unrestrained you kill a child
who attacked yet was not a danger
then unintentionally hack the innocent skull
of your newborn

※

a broken heart burned black and red
in the chest of a slit-throat mother
whose husband ran deranged
on the drugs of industry
to us it is a mystery

Gator Knowledge

The ground is alive
where vines crisscross
and dark green branches hang with moss
The omnivorous swamp doesn't care
whether you're living or dead
as it tears at your flesh
and hisses at your head
from the spirits' unseen bayou
Be ready, it is honest in its dread
Where we walk, we sing
within the living roots
in a timeless age
where laws are unnecessary
in the inheritance of culture
as respect is the only law
These locals know who they are
and share in their jubilant feast
with a giving eye on celebration with travellers
and a keen sense of where
it does and doesn't belong
Trees emerge from the walls and gutters
and red brick green with the eons of life
Rowdy are the galleries and balconies
as they have always been
and we look below, around, and above
where painted words remain
from when a mint julep was new
For that is not an old age in this place
where immortals frolic
over floods of shells
where slaves escaped
to freedom make
where generous witches and sea captains dine
on what they'll tell you is the best food
and they have a right to say it

Every meal is a new taste
new touches on every drink
The romance of anniversaries
lounging in a gondola on a lake
where on the bank an oak sings
and lips who match kiss under the bridge
The pirates are enlivened in the alley
which has never stopped
being stones for their feet
who have never stopped being wild and fleet
Wet and dripping is the music
where the gris gris stings right
in the vampire night
So, mix some red wine in your blood
and dance at the intersection of chaos and whimsy
Touch the midday slick brown water
of the river passing a voodoo offering
Give thanks and be merry
and feast forever
as fires holding the night

Poetry Trees

Underneath us all
is an exit
awaiting as the space under
scrolls of poetry hanging from trees,
yet it is not nothing.
It is the confluence of all that we have been
into the silent story of eternity
echoing, as above carries on
and we reemerge
into the whole.
Defy selling yourself.
Live your life,
explore, expand your welcome of the world.
Put down the filters;
you are rotting away
as you live in the past.
Self-exploitation has become a marketable skill.
Work, and live, with focused attention
and kindness.
It's been a long time since we really listened to music.
My environmental awareness
was almost gone.
If you're constantly seeking advice,
how can you hear your own logic,
your own thoughts?
Philosophy is thinking and questioning.
Poetry is being present,
truly present, fully.
I am alive with life.
Why would I stare into boredom
when I have a life to live?
I have more energy than ever.
We are so far from the founding discourse.
Rather than stare at your phone, meditate.
Rather than read a book, meditate,

but read books, too.
Rather than smoke, or drink,
or drug yourself into another world, meditate
and get there faster.
Hear the music of the universe,
live it, and don't stop living it.
Celebrate with the most natural therapy, dance.
You're lifting the weight of your own shadow.
You didn't notice, but now you can see.
Exemplify the uplifting freedom
and slip out of your casing
and fly.
We're taking our children
to our childhood homes.
We want them to know
and need them to know
who we are,
what we've seen,
the ordinary magic of the ancient world.
Get out there in the garden.
Discard addicting distraction
which carries you away from true delight.
Raise your arms up to the sun in the morn
and say to the one sea, "Thank you for making me!"

Day Use Manifesto

Good anger
seeping up in tears
against the injustice
caused by thieves
who buy and steal
what was once a natural miracle
and sell it back to travellers
while roping off wilder freedom.
All the way up
to the top of the mountain
posts bar the original destiny.
There is nowhere to go.
Stop business directing funds
into the executioners' hands
fencing off possibilities to roam
and corralling us like cattle
into trailer parks, mining camps,
subrural tent cities.
Day Use Only, No Camping
new white stickers on pointless barricades.
No fires, No coals
unless you pay for the right.
You've shoved and bullied
part of the ecosystem
out of the ecosystem
and now the barren dry lands
burn
and our safety in your concern
isn't open to compromise.
The laughing enforcers
slapping down your true home's access
to protect the river which has become roads.
We've been ushered into
the (planned) last resort
and set up camp

amidst sprinklers and vacuums
and carried our supplies
to the final green bank of pay-per-view land.
Stop funnelling resources
into things that don't work.
Cease engaging your emotions
in successful capitalism
and brainwashed families
who continue to behave
like violently ignorant goons.
I am calm
because we found a place
among the crowd.
But, I remember that good anger…

※

Wake up. Coffee.
Raise to the sky
soaking in the sunlight
and reaching to the earth
to stretch out all negativity
and bring the circle up, around,
and whole again.
Sage, cleanse.
Reflect. Meditate. Walk.
Bathe in the waterfalls of morning.
Read. Explore. Write.
Heat a wizard stew
with leftovers, new-overs
and carry a sun white cloud
in your vision.

Schemes and Alms

What were once
heinously rude invasions
of privacy are now entertainments.
Conversation is a rare ability
and most are tainted by agenda.
When opinions are presented
with facts to reason disagreement,
many will yell that only they can be right,
that facts have no bearing on consideration
and they #walkaway.
There is rarely a point in talking to people.
The connecting factors are more often missed
and the entirety is not seen.
Some abandon their own family
amidst consistent disasters,
some to travel the extreme left
and some the extreme right.
They are the same in their unwillingness to listen
and their destitute loyalties.
They preach acceptance, love, and inclusion
yet their self-centered minds make more enemies
and their ideals are hollow in their hatred.
We're not talking about those who do
or do not morally oppose violence,
but those who worship violence
as their flag's feet.
Commerce is a marketplace,
a public square owned by a few,
where everyone is holding their alms bowls
walking aimlessly.
With childhood's dreams in their memory,
they pander to the needs of none.
"I'll trade you one gold coin for a hazelnut."
replied to with a scheme
to trick them into trading more

and no one gets enough
or has enough to give,
but everyone goes home licking their coins
with contempt for their untraded goods.
There is now no mystery to the prostitutes.
They stand on the street (alone in their rooms)
waving their jiggling bodies at the world.
It seems everyone is terrified of boredom
and silence is almost unknown.
Imagination is drowned in thinking
and thinking is drowned in the electronics
telling you what you're thinking.
Looking at the world is strange to modern eyes.
Reading a book, anachronism.
But to wander in and wonder at
the wonder of nature inspires.
That is how Einstein's revelations
were thrust into the consciousness
of empires.

※

Arrive home to sweet pentacles on the mirror
from cute fingers and brushing teeth.
The nights of revelling are a sweet escape from the unreal
into reality.
Our friends are massing in the bowling alley where we
strike planets
and roll in joy
and have only enough patience with rudeness off center.
The mud and the fire and the water and the smoky air
mingle to be a cauldron of dancing and wandering.
Where our mothers are smiling at our happiness,
we shall one day be,
and continuing the turbulent rides,
madness crashing through each other,
we love on.
The water spirits gather in the morning
and laugh into the day
and pour onto their beloved earth
cuddling in a puddle of fearless love.
A wave throws the dust from their lives
and they wake and move and help and cheer.
While the morning is waking sleepily in clouds
and the breeze which began at dawn
to keep everyone inside,
the wild cusp children are speeding around the corners
clouding the story with their dust waves
and romantic freedom.

※

The first, beautiful day of the new year
you are free
Whatever you do, you are free

I was told my whole life I was sensitive
like it was a bad thing

You say I am sensitive
like it is a good thing
You could hear my passion
though I whispered in the wind
you who love me while you see
though I rage, my heart
You embrace the good in me
things I was told were flaws
and now I'm learning to embrace
who I'm allowed to be
and as I'm dealing with real flaws
which arise and must be fought
and relearning to quiet my mind
which says *yes* and *no* and screams
you teach the practicality
of functioning dreams

I have behaved wretchedly
In another, I'd despise
the wrongs which flew from hand and mouth
the dust from old loneliness
upon remaining pieces of a delusional puzzle
in the attic not fully cleaned out
Now, I will take this
and throw it away
Some things, like old hurts
belong in the trash
to make room for the new where you're healed

Outside the Rivergate

I see the top of the mountains
light up pink in the sunrise
and I think of you.
I walk along the river
flowing swift in the cold
and I am not cold
thinking of you.
The mountains have already prayed this morning
thankful for the day
smiling at the sun as it warms them.
We are in a tiny fraction
of the massive world
of high mountains and wide canyons
surrounding endless life.
I think of the happiest place on earth
and I think of you.
Watching the river
there is so much more water than man.
The water is patient.
It knows it can devour
all there is.
The water is patient
because it carries the invincible.
It is the invincible
and nowhere on earth can comprehend
the ultimate existence and transition
until they understand the way.
It is the same force with which I love you.

The Adventure Jacket

I wore the adventure jacket tonight
It's too small, but it fits
It fits with memory, my brother
It fits with adventure sans chagrin

Low Tide

The waves wash up slowly
the waves wash out slowly
let the baby clams tickle your feet
in the tide
I speak with a man in a local jeep
at the stoplight and he says,
"Life moves fast. You gotta take
every inch you can."
He looks happy and impatient
and drives up into the hills
the Kumeyaay jewels
of sunshine and cloud

※

There was a young man named Drew
who didn't know what to do.
He sat and did nothing,
nothing at all,
and that was the end of poor Drew.

※

The world
it is made for art
Otherwise, why
and who would care
It is the beauty of Life
unique expressions
Everyone comes to the river
in their own way
Yes, it is true, the journey
is forever full of changes
Who you are
is how you are
One day, you may have
a soft path to tread
An uneasy night may be brewing
dark, strange, and calm
When you awake
it is unfamiliar
Nowhere to step, you must crawl
over sharp, cutting rocks
Keep going
or you will die here
The mountain is infinite
to each their own journey
Though we meet at bonfire places
in the morning we disperse
We carry a key as we walk
creating our individual way
We can encourage and give guidance
to fellow selves on the way ascending
You will not help yourself
by harming another's tread
Find as you near…
where is the key?
The way appears as you breathe

and the summit grows brighter
You find that you are the way
smiling, remembering to be
Keep going, you are the key
to the entrance of the true Home

※

You can fly low
or you can fly high
not between where the people walk
desperate to find a cure for their boredom
and where the flags fly

Bàrd

poet, writer, historian
stargazer into eternity
storyteller, adventurer
ever-free of boundaries
diplomat, satirist, scholar
walking contradiction
music maker, song creator
soothseeker
and soothsayer
beyond the blood
to the sea
a bard is poetry

※

"Guru, would you rather be
a hammer or a nail?"

"I am the air between them.
I am the sparks when
the hammer strikes the railroad spike.
I am the heat of the day.
I am the man swinging the hammer
and the railroad being built.
I am the earth underneath."

※

The Sun is reborn.
My magic is reborn in the dawn.
It is foolishness to let others drag you into darkness
where you never wanted to be.
The birds know.
Everyday is the first day of the year.
The moon is so close, clear.
A raven flies with golden sunlight
on his feathers.

All the sky is sunrise!

All the sky is sunrise
after days of rain and shine
All the sky is sunrise
true lovers share its joy
All the sky is sunrise
none could be the poet's dear when
All the sky is sunrise
but they cannot see and hear
All the sky is sunrise
and fitting is the fear when
All the sky is sunrise
and in poetry disappears
All the sky is sunrise
and all but love is nothing
All the sky is sunrise
why let the hurt be in your mind
All the sky is sunrise
and joy is in your soul to find
All the sky is sunrise
and all the joy is mine

Books

Books are poetry
in themselves
I will not be one
who demands you know their enduring pleasure
There is no substitute
for discovery in pages
The feeling
as fleeting and real as feelings
as lasting, as obstinate
books are experience

※

Losing my mind
in mass dimensions
I think where I want to be
and the moment I open my window
to the morning
a flying *V* of geese
and tilted white paint-swept clouds
greet the brightening blue

Oh, an "artist"

- he said, oldly.
I smile, unharmed,
accustomed to belittlement,
accustomed to the attitudes of those
who disrespect creators, thinkers, and freaks
then go home to watch *Game of Thrones*.
One day, we will look at a star
and think of our friends living on that planet,
and who will have gotten us there?
The artistic thinkers.
The normal people will always
be just normal
while creators create the Universe.

※

I'm sorry I ever lashed out
desperate not to be forgiven
but to turn back time
to when I searched for a vixen
The scars of anger raise not cause
but effect
Violence does not teach respect
it only makes happy little boys and girls
cry because their father
is a miserable wreck

An American Flag

blindfold over eyes
above a big, gnashing mouth
with square yellow teeth.
In each hand, decapitated bodies
wrapped in American flag shrouds.
As blood drips down your jaws,
your arms,
their heads cry in your howls.
Your boasting bloodlust
and mindless love-melting
from an immutable source
to a red-hot liquid
transforms into weapons
what once was your heart.
You dread these words,
but you have no feet
and no foundation.
Your senses have been sucked from you
through the podiums which feed you poison
in exchange for your life.
You are nothing now
but an angry head, yellow teeth
and grips of death
with eyes replaced by stars and stripes,
an attacker, a dog
trained on any noise that,
when you growl,
does not say, "Yes, I agree."

Escape Artist

I am an old dragon
dreaming through realms
of time and imaginary
possibilities, endless
though seemingly sedentary
Chaos and cosmos
are merely two ordinary
borders between the center
and Infinite
and forever the dragon escapes

※

You are laying on the beach, ahi poke tacos, a rum drink
because you don't care about the sugar anymore
your husband biffing on his surfboard in the sunset

※

Spring open the windows
ye parents
wrecks of misery and perseverance
Ignore the children's dirty clothes
on the floor beside an empty
laundry basket
and the wet towels
flung far away from their hooks
This cannot delay your good day
but is part of the blessings you enjoy
as you recognize your cocoon
was your frustration at your cocoon
when you were meant to be emerging
no longer a caterpillar
but a fountain
of joy, ambassador of sunshine
kind, talented, happy and free
on the adventure of Life
bravery's perfume

※

He might leave work early
to walk in the hills with his kids
when the spring flowers carpet the earth.
That's the kind of person he was.
But, he might also yell like a maniac
feeling lost in clutter and injustice.
It must have been difficult to be him.
Once, a tiny teal grasshopper
appeared in the bonfire.
He quickly reached into the flames to save it,
but it was already burning.
It made him sad;
that baby grasshopper
was an actual baby burning alone in a house.
Finally, he let the desert sleep in him
and woke flowers.
Where are all those knights who won
their storied glory in battle?
A solitary man treads over
their rusted armor
on bombadillian paths of quiet
with bees buzzing around his ankles.

Dancing Over the Void

the art of joy
is the vision created
this, my home
loud with the league of extraordinary children
laughing and dancing with a gorgeous goddess wife
the twittling birds
from the trees, the house
the white picket fence surrounding a garden yard
the grassy field in sunshine
and beyond are the woods
which we explore
and mountains adventuring
where the sea visits and kisses the air
the cottage at the edge of a magic forest
writing, gardening, reading
an aura of immortality
a haven for green man and for the fae
where even the clatter of weapons
is a peaceful clatter
and the heroes, the witches
the happy wolves
champion eternity
by dancing over the void

※

Art is not defined by boundaries. Art is not bound by
definitions.
Art is contrary.
Art is the artist, yet it is beyond the artist. An artist is art, but
only sometimes.

※

Some people will enlist themselves
in a platoon of worthless banter
even though the most they do
is root for it from their ass
and give it their money
while learning the most pointless information
known to man.
Some people will treat contemptuously
the man
who while walking kindly closes
their mailbox
so their mail won't blow away,
or the person who is too slowly
walking across the road
delaying them for the time of one breath
from reaching their little tasks
which are ever more important
than everyone else's lives.
They could have been using that breath
to learn patience, to look inward, to see.
Instead, they used that breath
to drown in irritation.
How much do we go by
without seeing?

People in this age are obsessed
with labelling themselves and others.
There is no time of quiet,
which is required to think and discover.
They have replaced thinking with sharing.
They get their thoughts and prejudice
from a bowl of regurgitated soup
and want to be told the taste is correct.
I wonder if this is how the old world felt
watching christianity bloom in its death flower.
Death to consideration, to context,
conversation replaced with conversion.
Perhaps this is what happens
after an era of teaching the imperial authority
gained through genocide.
Their identifier is nothing more than a word
which is stuck on their face
and loudly defended
with the inability to recognize themselves,
turned to anger at lack of recognition.
"Validate my place in the world
at every shift of my mind!"
They want more than to be accepted
for their right to live as they please.
They demand all live in their reality,
all servants in reverence to their fantasy
and somehow, amidst deference
to their self-worship,
they demand to be given meaning,
to receive it as owed
for their blight of blessing
the world with their presence.
Your designation makes you defunct
because you are becoming the statue of a cause
fighting against other statues.
All classifications of advice
on how to fit in or fit out of society

perpetuate cultural drama,
even the popular rebellious flags.
You've just found a new fad.
A living soul requires no role.
The winter geese have returned to the north;
three black geese remain.
A dove flying, holding a twig
on its way to continue building a nest
is more of a religion
than all the religions combined.

Silent Lightning

To stand on a height
alone in the night
watching silent lightning
To feel nothing
one must be shuffling
so far within themselves
Up here at the tarn
where clouds are born
worry sheds in the breeze
To bowl through trapeze
of mouths to feed
patience brings joy to the free

Living Amongst the Wrong Tribe

I have to stop expecting
to be treated right by deserters
who expect everything and respect nothing.
I have to stop expecting.
Their greatest honoring of me
is for the shell of my soul.
They cling to each other on the earth
and leave me in the middle of the sea.
They cannot reciprocate my love.

A butterfly befriended of ants
tries to tell them the beauty of a flower
and share the connection with its eternal life,
but the colony will ask where's the best place
to begin tearing it away for food.
Alone the glider flies to the branch of a tree
and looks down upon the hill despondently,
over the world wonderingly
thinking in solitude's poetry
which they can but will not want to understand.
Others of its kind
fly higher in bright dreaming,
but it doesn't want to leave the ones
who would its wings tear apart
like a flower a breath after its passing
and take him down to their tunnels
to feast on his earthly being.

So, before he sinks awaiting them,
their kindness unreliable,
or fades among the chomping fangs
who disregard the visions of his brain,
he must remember the island in the sea
from which he came
and is destined to be;

invisible, maybe
like a deity
unreachable, always
except by the sea
and butterflies who live in dreams.

These friends, they say "Come!"
but when he grew legs and stepped out from the surf
they all turned away.
They want you to do something only for them;
that is how they treat mad spirits.
Yet you refuse their ways
and wonder why they don't include you in their play.

※

M oral
A mbiguity
G uiding
A mericans

The Mall

- is a sad place
abandoned, not transformed
what remains is the echoing of deserted tiles
what fun can be found is scraped from the edges
at the end of an empty civilization
archeologists won't need to dig
they can walk right in
but they'll walk right out again
because the only artifacts are glass doors
and they are all the same
buried in a sunlit grave
how long? ten years?
so quickly quiet of voices
even the aquarium is lonely
no swimming fish in the entryway
not because they have been freed
but because humans have become lazy
about beauty and fun
nothingness creeps out from behind the gorillas
in this place that cannot change
even the annoying kiosk vendors
would be comfort compared to this
where there were surrounded in laughter
the fountains of family and wishes
is silence, except the remains of bright signs
that still say 20% OFF
but there's nothing really left to buy
in this hub of drifting memory
of a people who had nothing to offer
the temple where they gathered in religion of purchase
the food court stands empty
with no beckoning smells
while sad, awake, angry
starting to realize it has been abandoned
the mall is becoming a monster

❉

smoke from the pagan fires
drifts through the purple night
under the streetlamp
through the branches of trees
the light reaching to you

The Princess's Birthday

Everywhere is made
brighter by your love
and your hands can
heal the world,
the magic hands
which summon sunflowers
where the gardener only meant peas.
Born of nature's freedom,
not blind to injustice or pain,
you wear the tartan colors
of the oldest bloodline,
daughter of gods, of kings and queens
with tresses thick as highland mist.
I let you believe
the fireworks were for you,
but I'll tell you at last
what is true; you
are the fireworks for us!

The Snore in a Desert of Temples

I love her soft snore.
Though in this land where temples to chosen fantasies
are built from the murdered living temples
we are drenched in sounds and images
and the quiet of a golden smiling sunset
is a rare escape,
we can return amidst the overcivilized din
to our gorgeous wilderness.
Denying the churches of recent ancestors
who were raised in an absence of history,
growing in a new age of neglect from those
who should have been their best teachers,
these new adolescents educated each other
in their ignorance
and fortified it with tartufferie.
Many of them would say they raised themselves,
isolated together in a night grove,
all of them alone
because all of them were talking
to anyone who would listen
without learning to listen to anyone.
No one taught them to hear good stories
and no one taught them to go outside
to play and dream for themselves.
Now, many elders are living as the younger ones,
trapped by their own isolation.
They went to the night grove of the lonely children
and have not returned.
Overstuffed with stimuli,
they do almost nothing but sit in gluttony
while their homes and hearts are barren.
They are learning from the lonely young
who educated themselves with wayward banter
and enforce their opinions without a foundation.
They who were meant to impart wisdom, continuity

as their children's sacred inheritance
are sitting in an old place of dead trees.
No story has meaning if it is only observed
and devoid of real living and being.
Diluted by opinions, they've forgotten stories
and labels are the depth of their context.
No one taught them to walk away in their minds
from someone's racist comment
or hateful ignorance
or consider a bit of information they don't want to hear,
no one taught them every difference of thought
is not World War III,
and so they walk away from their family.
Rebelling against elders who make religions of
opinionated fantasies,
the young howl with religious fervor
their lack of acceptance and their lack of
willingness to learn.
Not learning as drinking mindlessly
from an endless stream of gossip,
but learning as a real experience
away from our own disdain.
Throwing themselves into travel
without adventurous purpose,
for they learned from and continue to fill
a world with information,
they build now invisible temples
to their own egotistic exhibition.
Spoiled with things and starved of attention
by those who were
spoiled with answers and starved of seeking
by those who were
spoiled with identity and starved of sympathy…

In a desert of temples,
I return to her soft snore
and sink happily to bed.

A Moment of RAT-A-TAT-TAT!

In the land of the free
the proud eagle's flag
every day flies at half-mast
In the home of the brave
none are more so
than sweet children going to school
From sea to shining sea
mindswept victims
create new victims
Grappling with murder
Grappling with anger
Writing through desperate tears
of children's cries, children's blood,
scared sad children's faces
who'll be honored with silence
who'll be disgraced with silence

When a warrior's privilege
is every fool's right
you live in untrainable slaughter
When education is disrespected
and philosophy a nuisance
you live in continuous slaughter
When words and context
keep no meaning
you dwell in righteous slaughter
When hatred is foreign
but never domestic
you pray, and then you are slaughtered

※

When I say I hate
I am hurting from the stupidity of the cruel
family, friends, and the mass of evil
who laugh or yell or roll their eyes
when they cause pain.
So many foul-weather friends
wanted to join in misery
and gave up their role
when true smiling returned.
A scar of family deserting us
hurling disdainful rocks in our direction
after I salvaged their lifelong digressions.
I was always the golden child
until I spoke my mind.
They valued my honesty
unless I told pain
and it is this they refused to answer.
When I have not the skill to communicate
it is partly because
those who told me to try harder
interrupted harder and shouted over my voice
and went on ignoring me.
A quitter's words are heavy and meaningless.
The moment promises leave their lips
they fall to the ground.
So intent on proving immortals irrelevant
they refuse the love of the wild child
and watch but dare not embrace.
I learn to live my life.
In that is my best mood
not the grasping endless strife
which keeps me from good sight.
I have too much true work to do
though my work is disregarded
to let it be mired in desire

and pushing ego-drama to the fore
when the ancient forests of unicorn
in which I dwell do adore
my freedom spirit and fantasy mind
which never can halt for human kind.
Cruelty does not transfer here.
It has no currency.
Never will I forget their fear
in which they live and bark at needs.
Poets are ever wary
of mortal cares and gears.
So gather all our words since birth
and they equal the silence before.
All my best days were in another world
away from civilization's wreck
of civilization's wanting.
All talk and bravery
never matched their hearts' wishing
who live as sad self-worshipping slaves
to their image as false
as their image of god.
Fear in fame changing lyrics
to suit the offended cries
does not deserve the attention of ages
and yet and yet and yet…
the poets live on
while most of the most beloved gladiators
are dead and gone and forgotten.
Not useless do I make these forms
nor deprecate their worth.
But of all the varied norms
theirs was norm from birth.
They shit on souls and prance away
dropping the blame in their wake
their small-minded excellence
achieved with zero integrity.
The television warriors

place the bar of excellence
in the dirt where they sit
and still find a way to look up to it.
Social network reacts…
and they identify
as a conglomerate of voluminous waste.
Not as individuals
do they have the strength to act
nor with compassion
do they have the strength to speak.
Anonymous terrorists habitually cruel
without tact so accustomed
to dissatisfaction they demand it
of the proud and joyful
are the ones who create an anomaly
of uneducated cows
where none are needed yet they bellow
trying to prove their worth
and rale against the gem of birth.
They preach the cure to all misery
is to be a hardworking employee
to make a virtue of their weakness
while caring is strangled in the field.
They quit on their dreams
and take their self-righteous feigning
in pleasure giving advice
from where they live in thoughts
with a head full of lies
and a belly full only of what is convenient
deserting themselves before empty eyes
vomit on your life.
Did you ever notice quitters always have the answers?
You are fairytale royalty.
Stop expecting pitchfork-wielding idiots
to be your friends.
They twist your stories and your jokes
to match their wit's low measure.

No value in true friendship or the world
they must maim it like a churl.
They treat gifts from their friends
like garbage
and complain about the size of a pearl.
Those who do not care what is true
have no incentive to be honest with you.
You can be chieftain and do everything
to keep the ones you love together
yet some will contribute only
their absence.
This the person
this the emotional tie that binds.
Cut it
and be free of them.
They are nothing.
This desert suffocates thriving flowers
in its base heat and flawed logistics.
Here, the mediocre thrives
and the unhelpful chide
those who see over their walls
and, to rise above their gravity, fly.

But we arrived home
where the birds found their gift.
Among dusty bottles and pristine glasses
X marks the spot of our beach sand triumph.
Near the children's woad on a rock
in the frilly grass where they play
I've heard the trees' conversations
and the grumbling of the stone
eternity in the temporary
as this realm lives by change.
Even the gods cannot live here.
They can visit, but they cannot remain.
Otherwise they would die as we do
and thus we go to the realm everlasting.

Don't take this too seriously.
Religion is what happens
when we take things too seriously.
War is what happens
when we take things too seriously.
Stop letting your exhaustion
and your immature impatience speak.
Trust me, you do not want to break the hearts
of those who love you most.
Realize how much you've lashed out
with your insecurities.
Don't let your habits become addictions.
Choose your addictions
and go beyond them.
Overindulgence turns life's enjoyments
into poison.
Focus on your healthy obsessions,
love your healthy purpose,
and let it lead you to a happy life.
Deserts move, oceans move,
forests and mountains rise and spread
and crumble and recede.
Life is a story
and life is good.
Let's enjoy it.
Don't be stranded by your opinions.
Arborglyphs may lead the way
to a secret path in light.
Keep a sunset appointment with the sky
and keep a sunrise appointment.
I have seen the silver lining of the clouds
and it is as magical as the stories say.

※

Our gods are here.
If you stop, you can see
the trees waking up.
The mountains call to them
and they call back in the sunrise.
Some might see me walking,
a black cat in the rain,
but if you sensed my soul, you'd see
There! a dancing man.

※

At the height of autumn
and height of spring
the Tuath Lir in me
is tricked into thinking
this is somewhere I could live.
But, there is no reason to fear
my ambition made less than most
as I light my pipe and feign contentment
whether shivering or sweating
in this desert, this decomposing host.

※

I love the mist of Scotland
as it curls up from the bottle.
I've pulled the cork
and there it is,
the heady breath of the outlaw glen
where the smooth river bends.
Sometimes it tastes like home on my island,
sometimes cigar and bonfire.
This morning, it tasted like your mist,
primal respect to the sacred.

※

If poetry is the beating heart of America,
why do you seem surprised it's ignored?
How often is the beating heart attended
unless its bearer is sick?

※

Four times in a year
they say your words they'll buy
Yet never their friendly names
transparent lists do cry

※

They walked in the morning sun
to where a meteorite had landed
and picked it up to carry home from the stars.
They found brave sunflowers
growing amidst thorn trees;
they greeted the trees with nods
and went to the flowers
which raised up from a single stalk.
They spoke happily
and it made them feel welcome,
having found a way
to make this place home.

※

spit
   "You're too nice."
spit
   "You're too nice."
spit
   "You're too nice."

   "Stop spitting on me."

"You're not nice, anymore."
   walks away

To My Wife and My Kids

The sadness
of forever not belonging
is like long-fingered sharp claws
ripping me open to reveal
my real body

I have wasted so much of my life
on this sadness
and I dread how I have
made you feel
you who help me heal

No soul has ever loved as much
as my love grows for you
as poetry from the birth of rain
and the enlightening dew
as my heart learns from you

When those claws ripped through my mind
you have brought me back
with your smile and your voice
now a neverending pact
forever happy will I be
if I love me as I love you
and you love me as I love thee
you are the refreshing kiss of dew

※

I asked you to marry me
in my castle in the sea.
I've realized my castle
is wherever we are
you, me, and the league.

※

When the dooms of thought consume
my weary mind
then flowers bloom
of fortune's mistaken gloom
to find you here, and I your groom

This life of ever toils be
without you here
and the blesséd league
all my purpose living free
to adventure all, joyfully

Never can tears threaten us
for we always
chuckle and trust
and weave stronger patterns thus
which guard and give, outlive the dust

Renegades Together

"Why do they only love me
for a moment?"
asks the christmas tree
laying on the sidewalk.
"I don't know."
I respond, suppressing a tear
as I go on my way
and ponder.
Why did my mother
allow me and my brother
to be tortured as little children?
Whatever the reason,
it's not a good one.
So motherfuck them, tree.
Come back swinging.
Don't let them toss you out like garbage.
Motherfuck their labels.
I see you. Live
and burn on the streetsides.
We can be renegades together.
Show them the nature
their plain cement hides.
I've got some torch fuel.
I can help you.
But tree, don't die.

※

I might watch the sunrise
from my window every morn
but my wife with sniffling allergies
has starlight in her eyes.
It's hard to turn my gaze
a wolf in the trees
when her hair is not cooperating
and I'm lost in gorgeous waves.
Coffee and smiles, adoring her voice
and the words a queen might use
"tired" - "bloated" - wrapped in blankies
loving her beyond choice.

All I Ever Wanted To Be

- was a good daddy.
Yesterday, I was one of the worst
and any reasons I can find
do nothing to undo
the grind of screaming tears.
What is my success?
Happiness, that is what I saw
in my grandmother,
and what did it look like?
Kindness, gentle
quiet understanding,
patience, patience, patience…
As a child, I thought I was patient
because that is what I could see.
Not long after, I thought I was a monster
treated like an evil cat,
like a pagan among catholic converts

who needs imagination and fierce love
tortured out of him,
like a long-haired redskin at a whiteboys' school
where no one could understand my spirit,
like a dark poet pelted with rocks
because I could not and would not
speak dull language,
a rootless rebel refusing a cause
unless it be universal freedom,
but, loving, find that it was always true
and thus is lost and demonized.
Now, I must work to eschew
past trauma which makes one vindictive
and determine to be true to myself,
not the pain inflicted.
I do not deserve forgiveness
for the recurring, unconscious harm.
But, if you do return to my arms,
I will know I am the luckiest,
I will take this monster into the woods,
kill him and reborn remain
smiling, the best, the way you remember me,
all I ever wanted to be,
a good daddy.

※

Just seeing a bird fly to its home
in the branches in a tree
in the sherbet sunset
recalled my terror
away and me
to the forest
of imagining

※

parenting's hard
go to the park
eat fresh
restore the zest
don't rhyme
unless you have time

※

Rage,
rage against the dying of the might
like Fenius Hero of Oceans
braved the waves of flooded plight
For the destruction of the Mother Goddess
saddened by her holy tribe's
divine ignorance
was a wrath of renewing

So, Tolkien's Oxford
catch'd a goblin
outside their door
How 'bout dat?
Desperate to be relevant
they lose their purpose
and enact a controlled burn
of the Library
It is they who
masturbating in the corridors
are caught among the tomes
and torn from the world
by the fiery pages
they rejected for the new

Play and rage
be total above the murder of the day
for only those who live this way
endure

※

I repeated a Jim Crow joke
and my friend smiled
because white people are "crazy"
but I've recently learned
about the guileful smile
and I hope he forgives me
I hope he doesn't lock me
in the cage of his hate
for I will never be there
but he will resent me

1ˢᵗ 3ʳᵈ 6ᵗʰ Anniversary

"She…" is terribly cliché
so I won't start a poem this way
unless it's with humor written for
an amazing wife-goddess-queen
because I want you to have everything

a person is a poem

a person is a poem
when they laugh or they cry
a person is a poem
no need to ask why
a person is a poem
outgoing or shy
a person is a poem
that may never die
a person is a poem
which can change in an instant
a person is a poem
and a person can fly

※

Bad friends are like
weak coffee

…why

※

sushi from the sea
chopsticks from trees far away
elemental feast

※

From a walk in the sand
to Disneyland
From a glass slipper
to a wedding dress zipper
The rain reveals the clue
I have finally found you

lowercase manifesto

a poet is a murderer

of predictability
and never lets you abound
in comfortable silence
without giving an opportunity to wreck it with depth
and expand it through language

poetry is because poets breathe
and speak what would be without poets

with veins of magic
poets see
that which poetry
sees

there is nothing it has to do
and nothing it can't do
for it is the breathing of Life

※

His father beat him with a bible
but I need not forgive him
He twisted my brother's mind and mine
and taught us pain and hate

His father punched him to shut him up
I suppose I should forgive him
But that little boy grew to be a bully
and punished us all with his hate

... but if we had no art

the houses would crumble
the castles and stories
with the pagan king would shy
though he takes the last of nothing for himself
all the heart would be unseen
the pagan princess gives and heals
but if we had no art
their ancient line would be no lore
there'd be only creeds of kill
I see what the pagan prince has built
a slope which ramps to dreams
victory is living a life you love
but if we had no art
pagan royalty would cease
and as yet
it has not

Inciteful Prayer

Earth's murder-minded Muslims, Jews, and Christians
need to get the fuck over yourselves
and see the inspiration to live
as if your own lives matter

When one man does it
it's called theft and murder
and when thousands of men do the same
it's called civilization

Complete this wholly unoriginal war
and jump to conclusions of grandeur
and in the time it takes to return
to childhood's dream, you'll be more

Yes it has been raging since the ancients
battled through oceans of fame
and then it was foolish as now it is ghoulish
to call greed by any other name

To live as if the world is yours
to demand and direct at your pleasure
and to villainize any who speak not your tongue
prove the ignorant cultureless-tethered

They'll make you think
you must choose a side
and in their hatred
their un-life, they lie

End this who are not at the Hot Gates
defending their home from invaders
and see that tribes have always been meant
to explore and to share and to change

Bravery

- is as important as a good fire
clean dishes
someone who loves you

※

a good decision is felt
at the arrival of the winter geese
and I return inside to live the right life

※

How long are you going to stare into that darkness?
It's simple; if sadness is upon you
or confusion or terror
if you feel devoid of emotion or thought
walk through it
as serenely as you can.
We add a new rung
to our depression ladder
as if punishing ourselves
for our sadness.
Discard the ladder
remember you can fly
and dance over the void.

www.ingramcontent.com/pod-product-compliance
Lightning Source LLC
Chambersburg PA
CBHW070013100426
42741CB00012B/3224